George Orwell's
ANIMAL FARM

NOTES

A CONTEMPORARY
LITERARY VIEWS BOOK

Edited and with an Introduction by
HAROLD BLOOM

5 7 9 8 6 4

Library of Congress Cataloging- in-Publication Data

George Orwell's Animal Farm / edited and with an introduction by Harold Bloom
p. cm — (Bloom's reviews)
Includes bibliographical references and index.
Summary: Includes a brief biography of the author, thematic and structural analysis of the work, critical views, and an index of themes and ideas.
ISBN 0-7910-4077-1 (hc) — ISBN 0-7910-4110-7 (pbk)
1. Orwell, George, 1903-1950. Animal Farm. [1. Orwell, George, 1903-1950. Animal farm. 2. English literature—History and criticism.]
I. Bloom, Harold. II. Series.
PR6029.R8A63 1995
823'.912—dc20
95-45111
CIP
AC

Chelsea House Publishers
1974 Sproul Road, Suite 400
P.O. Box 914
Broomall, PA 19008-0914

Contents

User's Guide

This volume is designed to present biographical, critical, and bibliographical information on George Orwell and *Animal Farm*. Following Harold Bloom's introduction, there appears a detailed biography of the author, discussing the major events in his life and his important literary works. Then follows a thematic and structural analysis of the work, in which significant themes, patterns, and motifs are traced. An annotated list of characters supplies brief information on the chief characters in the work.

A selection of critical extracts, derived from previously published material by leading critics, then follows. The extracts consist of such things as statements by the author on his work, early reviews of the work, and later evaluations down to the present day. The items are arranged chronologically by date of first publication. A bibliography of Orwell's writings (including a complete listing of all books he wrote, cowrote, edited, and translated, and selected posthumous publications), a list of additional books and articles on him and on *Animal Farm,* and an index of themes and ideas conclude the volume.

Harold Bloom is Sterling Professor of the Humanities at Yale University and Henry W. and Albert A. Berg Professor of English at the New York University Graduate School. He is the author of twenty books and the editor of more than thirty anthologies of literature and literary criticism.

Professor Bloom's works include *Shelley's Mythmaking* (1959), *The Visionary Company* (1961), *Blake's Apocalypse* (1963), *Yeats* (1970), *A Map of Misreading* (1975), *Kabbalah and Criticism* (1975), and *Agon: Towards a Theory of Revisionism* (1982). *The Anxiety of Influence* (1973) sets forth Professor Bloom's provocative theory of the literary relationships between the great writers and their predecessors. His most recent books are *The American Religion* (1992) and *The Western Canon* (1994).

Professor Bloom earned his Ph.D. from Yale University in 1955 and has served on the Yale faculty since then. He is a 1985 MacArthur Foundation Award recipient and served as the Charles Eliot Norton Professor of Poetry at Harvard University in 1987–88. He is currently the editor of the Chelsea House series Major Literary Characters and Modern Critical Views, and other Chelsea House series in literary criticism.

Introduction

HAROLD BLOOM

One critic remarked of George Orwell that he wrote sympathetically about human beings only when he presented them as animals. The truth of this can be tested by comparing *Animal Farm* to *Nineteen Eighty-four;* Napoleon (Stalin) is preferable to the torturer O'Brien, perhaps because even a whip-wielding boar is more tolerated by Orwell than a sadistic human. Poor Boxer, the martyred workhorse, is certainly more lovable than Winston Smith, and Mollie the flirtatious mare is more charming than poor Julia. Orwell's dislike of people resembles that of a much greater moral satirist, Jonathan Swift: Each loved individual persons, while despising mankind in the mass. Whatever the aesthetic flaws of *Animal Farm,* it seems to me a better book than *Nineteen Eighty-four,* primarily because it allows us a few animals with whom we can identify. Even Benjamin, the ill-tempered old donkey, silent and cynical, and incapable of laughing, still becomes somewhat dear to us, largely because of his devotion to the heroic Boxer. I'm not certain that I don't prefer Snowball (Trotsky) to anyone at all in *Nineteen Eighty-four,* because at least he is vivacious and inventive.

The great Canadian critic Northrop Frye observed that *Animal Farm* adapts from Swift's *A Tale of a Tub* the classical formula of much literary satire: "the corruption of principle by expediency," or the fall of Utopia. Unlike Swift, however, as Frye again notes, Orwell is not concerned with motivation. The reader is not encouraged to ask: What does the inscrutable Napoleon-Stalin want? Orwell's point may be that absolute power is desired by tyrants simply for its own sake, but *Animal Farm* hardly makes that very clear. The beast-fable is a fascinating genre, but it demands a certain psychological clarity, whether in Chaucer or in Thurber, and *Animal Farm* mostly evades psychological categories.

Orwell essentially was a liberal moralist, grimly preoccupied with preserving a few old-fashioned virtues while fearing that the technological future would only enhance human depravity. *Animal Farm,* like *Nineteen Eighty-four,* retains its relevance because we are entering into a computerized world where a post-Orwellian "virtual reality" could be used as yet another betrayal of individual liberty. Part of the residual strength of *Animal Farm* is that we can imagine a version of it in early twenty-first century America in which all the "animals" will be compelled to live some variant upon a theocratic "Contract with the American Family." Perhaps the motto of that theocracy will be: "All animals are holy but some animals are holier than others." ♣

Biography of George Orwell

George Orwell was the pseudonym of Eric Arthur Blair, who was born on June 25, 1903, in Motihari, Bengal, the son of a minor British official in India. When Orwell was two he returned to England with his mother and older sister. The family was able to save enough money to send their only son to St. Cyprian's, an expensive private school near Eastbourne. There Orwell won scholarships to Wellington and, in 1917, to Eton, where he spent four years. Although an excellent (albeit unhappy) student at St. Cyprian's, Orwell showed little interest in his studies at Eton. Instead of going on to university like most of his classmates, he became an officer in the Burmese Imperial Police.

Orwell's five years in Burma were dismal. In his first novel, *Burmese Days* (1934), he painted a highly critical portrait of the British community there. In 1927 he returned to England, penniless and without prospects. For several years he lived in London and then Paris, earning only enough money to feed himself. His experiences among the world of day laborers, itinerant hop-pickers, and restaurant employers were chronicled in his first published book, *Down and Out in Paris and London* (1933).

Although his early ambition was to write "a neat shelf of realistic novels," Orwell's growing involvement in political debate impinged more and more on his literary career as the 1930s progressed. Following two minor novels (*A Clergyman's Daughter*, 1935, and *Keep the Aspidistra Flying*, 1936), he was commissioned in 1936 to write a book-length report on the living conditions of miners in the north of England. This study was published by the Left Book Club as *The Road to Wigan Pier* (1937). The following year Orwell went to Spain to cover the civil war there, and wound up as a captain in the military arm of a syndicalist party fighting against the Falangist insurgents. After many months at the front he was shot through the neck, sustaining a permanent injury to his vocal chords, and returned behind the lines just in time to find that his faction had been denounced by its Communist partners and was being systematically purged. With his wife of one year, Eileen O'Shaughnessy, he escaped across the border to France and returned to England, where he published *Homage to Catalonia* (1938), an account of his Spanish adventure.

In 1939 Orwell published a fourth novel, *Coming Up for Air,* and continued to write political commentary and reviews. Once World War II broke out he joined the Home Guard and began to work for the BBC in its Indian Division, producing presentations of political and literary commentary for broadcast in India. (These pieces were later published in 1985 as *The War Broadcasts* and *The War Commentaries.*) In 1943 he left that position after disputes with his superiors over the censorship of war news and took a position as literary editor of the *Tribune,* a left-wing weekly where he also wrote a column for several years entitled "As I Please." During this time he also composed a brief satirical fable about Stalinism, which after many rejections was published in 1945 as *Animal Farm.* In the same year his wife died suddenly, leaving the chronically ill Orwell to raise their adopted infant son.

Increasingly hampered by pneumonia, Orwell spent his final years on the Outer Hebrides island of Jura, working on his last novel, *Nineteen Eighty-four* (1949). This bitter and compelling dystopian fantasy of the ultimate totalitarian future was an immediate worldwide success, but Orwell failed to live long enough to reap its rewards. After entering a London hospital for treatment of his tuberculosis in late 1949, he married a young editorial assistant, Sonia Brownell, in a bedside ceremony. A month later, on January 21, 1950, he died following severe hemorrhaging in one lung.

In his short life George Orwell managed to leave several works that would inspire and define debate across the politicial spectrum for decades following. He is also regarded as among the finest essayists in modern English literature, and his *Collected Essays, Journalism and Letters* appeared in four volumes in 1968. ✤

Thematic and Structural Analysis

The animals on Manor Farm find themselves in dire straits as George Orwell begins his tale of revolution and its aftermath. Mr. Jones, the despotic owner of this farm, works his animals extremely hard without paying proper attention to their needs for food or rest. On the day that the story opens, the animals have been summoned to meet by Old Major, a venerable boar well respected for his wisdom. As word of the meeting spreads among the animals, it is learned that Old Major has had a special dream that he wishes to recount to them after Mr. Jones has gone to bed.

Quietly, all the animals enter the confines of the barn and take their places in front of Old Major. Three dogs, Bluebell, Jessie, and Pincher, come in first. Then the pigs enter and seat themselves together. Boxer and Clover, the two cart horses, enter as well. These are followed by Muriel, the goat. Benjamin the donkey, the oldest and grumpiest animal, also comes in. Next, Mollie, the spoiled mare of Mr. Jones, squeezes in near the front of the group. All the animals, even the cat, are present inside the barn, except Moses, the tame raven. Thus, in the **first chapter,** Orwell uses the gathering in the barn in two ways: first, the procession of animals serves as their snapshot introduction, and second, Old Major's message for the future sets the tone for the animals' campaign for liberation. Major begins his speech not about his dream but about the general state of the animals' life on the farm. He believes that his time with them is short, so he must impart to them the learning of his years. In doing this, Major points out the obvious: their life is one of misery and slavery. Major further states that this condition is not part of the natural order; rather, as Major notes, Man is responsible for the animals' plight. Here Major explains that Man, at the expense of the animals under his care, is the only creature that consumes without producing. Man takes the offspring of the animals, for sale or consumption, and exploits the abilities of the animals until they are no longer of use. Only by eliminating Man from their lives can the animals rid the evils from their life on the farm. Only then would the product of their labor once again be their own. Major's message is simple: The animals must rebel against Man. Their struggle against Man must unite them, whether they are farm animals or wild creatures. And so, their first dictum evolves: Whatever walks on two legs is the enemy; whatever has four legs or has wings is a friend. Major admonishes them further by saying that under no circumstances should they adopt the ways of Man; that is, the animals should never live in a house, wear clothes, drink alcohol, nor deal with money or trade. Most important of all, no animal should ever control or kill another animal because all animals are equal.

At this point, Major recounts the dream that has brought all the animals together. In the dream, Major has seen a world without Man. This vision reminds him of a song he learned when very young. Though old and quite hoarse now, Major sings the verses of *Beasts of England* for the animals. Their excitement is uncontained when they hear the stirring lyrics. Soon all are singing along with Major until their joyous sound wakens Mr. Jones. Thinking a fox is near, Mr. Jones grabs his gun and shoots it. The shot spreads as it hits the wall of the barn, startling and scattering all the animals. They return, as the first chapter ends, quickly and quietly to their places on the farm, which is soon surrounded in silence.

Chapter two begins with Old Major's death. Much activity follows his burial. The animals begin to unite their efforts under the tutelage of the pigs, who act as the principal organizers. Three in particular stand out. Snowball, a young boar, is vivacious, a quick speaker, and quite inventive. Napoleon is distinguished from all others because he is the only Berkshire boar on the farm. He usually gets his own way although he is not as much of a talker as Snowball. Squealer, a small fat pig, is the most adept talker of them all. It has been said that when talking Squealer can turn black into white. Taking Old Major's words, these three have developed a philosophy that they call Animalism, which they teach to the other animals in secret meetings held after Mr. Jones has gone to sleep. At first, the pigs meet with great difficulty, either because of stupidity or apathy, or just because the other animals have been under the control of Mr. Jones for so long. Mollie, the white mare, is only concerned with sugar and ribbons for her mane. Moses, the raven, works against the pigs by telling tales, spying, and talking of a mythical Sugarcandy Mountain where animals go when they die. The pigs do find two allies in the cart horses, Boxer and Clover, who, although they are very slow learners, accept everything their teachers tell them.

Despite these initial difficulties, the Rebellion actually happens sooner than expected. For some time, Mr. Jones and his workers had been neglecting the farm and the animals. One night, at the end of a particularly idle day, Mr. Jones goes to town without feeding the animals. Later, he returns quite drunk and goes to sleep immediately, leaving the animals unfed. One cow has had enough and breaks through the wall of the grain shed with its horns. All the animals hurry to help themselves to the grain. Suddenly Mr. Jones wakes up and notices the commotion. He and his men run toward the animals with whips at the ready. Though they had not planned it ahead of time, the animals unite in an attack against Mr. Jones and his men. Quite unexpectedly, the men find themselves being chased through the gate by the animals. In the meantime, Mrs. Jones sees the attack, grabs a few things, and hurries out of harm's way. Before they know it, the animals have realized their dream: They have driven off the humans and are in possession of the farm.

Their first act of triumph is to remove all traces of Man from the farm. Thus the animals gather up the harnesses, whips, chains, knives, and all other instruments of Man's cruelty. They throw these things upon a great pile that becomes a celebratory bonfire. As they watch the fire burn, the animals sing their anthem with great joy. Then all retire to their sleeping quarters for a well-deserved night's sleep. The next day, the animals wake to the realization of their glorious triumph. They march around the perimeter of the farm to survey all that is theirs. They also tour the inside of the farmhouse and see all the trappings of Man's life there that had been acquired at their expense.

Next, Napoleon and Snowball call their first meeting. There is much to do, they announce, since the hay harvest is to begin.

At the meeting, the pigs reveal that they have taught themselves to read and write since Old Major's death. With paint and brush, Napoleon and Snowball go to the front gate. There Snowball cross out "Manor Farm" and paint "Animal Farm," which is to be the new name of their farm. Then, returning to the barn, the pigs explain that they have established seven rules based on Animalism. Snowball paints the Seven Commandments on the barn wall in great white letters. The last of these commandments reads: "All animals are equal." Just as the pigs are about to send everyone to the field to start the harvest, the cows who have not yet been milked start to low. With some difficulty, the pigs manage to milk them and thus put them at ease. When someone asks what will become of the milk that Mr. Jones used to sell, Napoleon diverts the animals' attention from the milk back to the hay harvest. But by the time the animals return that night from the fields, the milk has disappeared.

Chapter three describes the initial results of the animals' hard work. Their first harvest is a greater success than had been expected. To accomplish this, the animals have worked hard at what they know and have improvised in the tasks more suited to humans. All this work has been carried out under the direction of the pigs. The animals are careful not to waste anything. They take great pleasure in their labor, since they now directly enjoy the results of it. They call each other "comrade" as Old Major had taught them to do. Even though the tasks at hand are arduous, the animals soon enjoy more food and leisure time than they have ever known. In particular, on Sundays all rest from their labors. The animals take a late breakfast and then observe the Sunday ritual of hoisting their new flag, attending the weekly meeting, and singing the anthem. At the meetings, the work for the coming week is discussed. The pigs always suggest what should be done, and the others vote in agreement. Some of the pigs' projects meet with failure, but, in general, the reading and writing classes progress well. The pigs and the dogs can read, though not all showed an interest. Clover and Boxer have difficulty even mastering the alphabet. The slower animals—the sheep, the hens, and the ducks—cannot read and have trouble memorizing the Seven Commandments, so Snowball reduces the seven to the maxim:

"Four legs good, two legs bad." Napoleon does not pay as much attention to teaching as did Snowball. Instead, he focuses on the new pups born to Jessie and Bluebell. He takes the pups away and keeps them in seclusion until most of the animals forget about them. Gradually, it becomes known that the disappearing milk was going into the pigs' mash. Later, the windfall apples are delivered to the pigs' headquarters. Squealer is sent out to explain that the pigs need the extra nourishment because they alone are responsible for the directions and the organization that keep the farm going, meaning, too, that the pigs keep Mr. Jones far away. None of the other animals can dispute this fact.

In **chapter four,** the humans attempt to strike back. Since the Rebellion, Napoleon and Snowball have regularly sent out pigeons to carry the word of the animals' triumph across the farms and the countryside. Gradually, animals on other farms hear of the success of Animal Farm and also learn to sing *Beasts of England.* In the meantime, Mr. Jones consoles himself at the Red Lion tavern and tries to garner the sympathy of the other farmers. At first, the farmers do not pay much attention until their own animals, encouraged by the messages sent out from Animal Farm, begin to act out. Then, the same pigeons that had carried the word of rebellion and triumph return one day to warn the animals that the humans have armed themselves and are approaching the front gate. Anticipating just such an event, Snowball has devised a plan based on his studies of the campaigns of Julius Caesar. The animals launch a two-phased attack: The first lets the humans think they were victorious, while a second routs all humans from Animal Farm. There are casualties; however, triumph once again belongs to the animals. They raise their green flag, sing their anthem several times, and give their fallen comrades a fitting funeral. They also bestow their first military honors on Snowball and Boxer for their heroic participation in the battle. In the future, the animals decide to commemorate the day, called the Battle of the Cowshed, with the same honors as the anniversary of the Rebellion.

Despite their success against difficulties from without, those caused from within begin to divide the animals more dramatically in **chapter five.** The first symptom of trouble is seen in Mollie, the spoiled and lazy mare. Her comrades accuse her not only of not sharing her workload but also of speaking to one of the men from the neighboring farm. Shortly after the confrontation, Mollie disappears. Some time passes before the pigeons return to report that Mollie has been seen sporting a new scarlet ribbon and eating sugar from the hand of a man. The animals never speak of Mollie again.

The weather provokes further symptoms of difficulty. The winter is quite hard. Since little work can be done outside, frequent meetings are held in the barn to discuss future plans for the farm. By now, the pigs run both the meetings and the organization of the farm. The other animals have recognized that the pigs are the most able, and consequently have agreed to allow the pigs to make all decisions, later ratified by a majority vote by all animals. But the friction between Napoleon and Snowball disturbs what might have been a good working system. These two have radically different strategies. Snowball studies farm journals and delivers stirring speeches at the meetings. Because of his eloquence, Snowball is able to convince the animals to support his ideas. Napoleon, on the other hand, rarely speaks at the meetings or introduces new ideas. Rather, he rallies support privately by appealing to the slower animals and by questioning the success of any plan put forth by Snowball.

The plan that brings the rivalry to a head concerns the building of a windmill. Although the construction would be very difficult, Snowball explains, the windmill will introduce long-term benefits to the farm, resulting in shorter work weeks and better living conditions. Napoleon, commenting only in private, opposes the plan from the beginning. By the time Snowball presents the plan, the farm animals have formed two camps of support. But Snowball's stirring description of the future that awaits them encourages the animals to such a point that all are on the verge of voting acceptance. Just then, out of nowhere, Napoleon summons nine fierce dogs who attack Snowball and chase him off the farm. Stunned by the suddenness of the violent attack, the animals now direct their attention to Napoleon. The nine dogs sitting beside him reinforce his new role.

Napoleon disbands the Sunday meetings, announcing that all decisions will now be made by a committee of pigs that he would lead. There is dissent among the animals, but none feels able enough to articulate any objections, and the presence of the dogs now guarantees obedience. Squealer is sent out, as soon becomes the custom, to explain the new order, including, as it turns out, Napoleon's new mandate for the construction of a windmill.

The next chapters concentrate on life on Animal Farm after Napoleon's rise to power. In **chapter six,** several disquieting changes occur that cause concern and doubt among the animals. First, the new work regime is rigorous. The animals work sixty hours a week. Soon, Napoleon introduces voluntary work on Sundays as well, with the stipulation that if an animal does not volunteer, his food ration will be halved. But despite the extra hours, the weather that spring and summer allows the animals to complete their farm chores and to work on Napoleon's windmill. The shortages in some of the supplies, however, go unexplained. Next, Napoleon makes an unsettling announcement. He has decided to trade with Man in order to acquire tools and supplies needed for the windmill's construction. Squealer is soon dispatched to squelch the animals' complaints. To the animals' comments that this activity is forbidden, Squealer craftily questions their memory and suggests that the traitor Snowball is probably responsible for such an uncooperative attitude. Then, to make matters worse, the pigs move into the farmhouse to live. When the animals quote the Fourth Commandment, "No animal shall sleep in a bed," Squealer once again uses his cunning to turn the animals around. He asks Muriel, the white goat, to read the Commandment, which now conveniently reads, "No animal shall sleep in bed with sheets." The work and the harvest keep the attention of the animals from questioning the pigs' decisions any further. In the autumn, the harvest is in and the mill is half finished, and they are content. Once again, however, the weather brings the already tense situation to a head. A violent storm comes up with such strong winds that overnight the windmill is destroyed. Looking at the ruins the next day, Napoleor accuses Snowball of sabotage and pronounces a death sentence on him in front of a gathering of very startled and confused animals.

In **chapter seven,** the weather continues to be a factor. A bitter winter makes the construction of the new windmill even more arduous. Food rations diminish rapidly, threatening starvation. Then, Napoleon announces that he has made arrangements with Mr. Whymper, a solicitor from town, to sell eggs. The hens revolt, but Napoleon wins out after issuing threats to both the hens and any animal aiding them. Snowball continues to be used as the excuse for anything that goes wrong on the farm. Finally, one day, Squealer appears to announce that Snowball has been sighted on a neighboring farm and is known to be plotting against Animal Farm. In fact, Squealer maintains, Snowball had conspired with Mr. Jones to assist in the defeat of the animals at the Battle of the Cowshed. The animals are perplexed. Their memory of Snowball's brave action in the battle does not coincide with Squealer's vicious accusations. Squealer insists that Napoleon has proved categorically that Snowball is a conspirator and traitor. Squealer warns that all animals should be on guard against Snowball. Then, some days later, Napoleon calls a meeting where he accuses four young pigs and some of the hens of conspiring with Snowball. Napoleon's nine guard dogs tear their throats out in front of the other animals, who by now have been scared into complete submission to Napoleon's desires.

In **chapter eight,** Napoleon's position as leader is further reinforced. Squealer is now the official spokesman for Napoleon, who rarely appears in public. But despite his personal absence, his presence is felt everywhere. Napoleon now is always referred to as Comrade Napoleon. A poem written in his honor is set to music and replaces the anthem, *Beasts of England*. At the same time, Napoleon enters into business negotiations directly with Frederick, a neighboring farmer. Word of this spreads quickly among the animals because Frederick has such a terrible reputation for his brutal treatment of animals. Squealer once again smooths over the controversy by maintaining that Napoleon would never trade with Frederick. To make the animals feel better, their slogan "Death to Humanity" is changed to "Death to Frederick." Then, by dint of all the hard work and sacrifices made by the animals, they complete the windmill by the deadline imposed by Napoleon. But their celebration is abruptly cut short when the animals find out that, after all, Napoleon had gone ahead with the business deal with Frederick. Napoleon has planned this all along, contending that the rumors of Frederick's ill-treatment of his animals and impending attack are unfounded; that, in fact, Snowball is responsible for the gossip, and that by pretending to deal with another farmer, Napoleon was able to extract a much higher price from Frederick. The other pigs are delighted.

Napoleon gloats in his victory over Man and even shows off the money at the next meeting. But his boasting is interrupted by the news that Frederick's bank notes are forgeries. Napoleon pronounces a death sentence on Frederick, who, as it turns out, is entering the front gate with fifteen other men at the ready. Without prior planning on the animals' part, this battle is not as successful as the Battle of the Cowshed. The men wound or kill many of the animals. The remaining animals hide from the attack in the barn; there they watch, to their horror, the men explode the windmill that represents such long and hard work. The subsequent rage felt by the animals is enough to propel them once again against the men. Although there are significant casualties on both sides, the animals are finally able to drive the men from the farm. Squealer is dispatched to announce a victory celebration, at which time Napoleon awards himself new military honors.

In **chapter nine**, however, Boxer still has not recovered from his wounds suffered at what Napoleon refers to as the victorious Battle of the Windmill. For a third time, the animals start the construction of the windmill, with Boxer, as before, faithfully working more than his years or his health should allow. In the meantime, life for the animals continues to be hard as a result of the weather and short rations. But, at the same time, life for the pigs improves with each day. The pigs receive special rations, including cooked barley. Any other animal meeting with a pig must now step aside to let the pig pass. As well, Napoleon, having fathered many new piglets, decides that Animal Farm needs to build a school. So any money is directed to purchase bricks and mortar, instead of more food for the animals. Nevertheless, the animals are led to believe that their life is more dignified now than it ever was with Mr. Jones. Now they have songs, speeches, and processions; and at the same time, so much has happened that most of the animals barely remember how life was with Mr. Jones. Animal Farm is declared a republic, and Napoleon is elected president by a unanimous vote. Boxer's health, however, does not improve. Squealer tells the animals that because Napoleon is so concerned for Boxer he will have Boxer sent to the hospital. This news does not calm the animals, however, since the hospital is run by Man. Squealer succeeds in assuaging their fears until the day the men come to take Boxer away. Benjamin, always contrary and independent, screams at the other animals when he notices the sign on the truck. Napoleon has not arranged to take Boxer to the hospital; rather he is being carried off to the slaughterhouse. As usual, Squealer steps in to calm the animals. Some days later, Squealer calls the animals together to tell them of Boxer's death in the hospital. Squealer recounts Boxer's supposed last words—as Squealer remembers them, that is.

As **chapter ten** opens, several years have passed and the memory of life before the Rebellion is now quite dim. Things have improved on the farm. Two more fields have been purchased. The windmill now functions but is used to mill corn for profit instead of generating electricity as Snowball once had envisioned. The farm produces a steady income, although the food rations have improved only for the pigs and the dogs. But for the other animals, life continues as it always seems to have. The hope for a better life is still alive because, after all, theirs is the only farm in England that is run by animals. Even the anthem, *Beasts of England,* still fills the imagination of the animals, although none dares to sing it. Other things have changed also. Squealer, for example, is seen walking on two legs and carrying a whip. The slogan of the sheep has changed from "Four legs good, two legs bad" to the new version of "Four legs good, two legs better." And when Clover asks Benjamin to read him the Seven Commandments from the barn wall, Benjamin realizes in horror that now there is only one Commandment: "All animals are equal, but some animals are more equal than others." One final change is noticed. At a reception given in the farmhouse by the pigs for the neighboring farmers, the pigs and the men sit down at the same table to enjoy a feast of food and drink. During the meal, the men salute the success of Animal Farm, but Napoleon lets them know that the farm is now called Manor Farm. While playing cards after dinner, both Napoleon and a farmer play the same card simultaneously. Shouts of anger fill the air, and when the animals observe the dispute they look from pig to man, then from man to pig, and can no longer see a difference between the two. ✤

—Elizabeth Beaudin
Yale University

List of Characters

Mr. Jones is the man who owns and operates Manor Farm. He has a reputation for treating his animals badly by working them too hard and feeding them too little. He tends to be lazy and to drink too much. After losing the farm to the animals, he rallies support from the other farmers, including Mr. Frederick and Mr. Pilkington, to regain the farm. Their attempt, however, is unsuccessful. Mr. Jones represents Man to the animals, the enemy that they hate and fear.

Moses, the tame raven, has the reputation of spying for Mr. Jones. What is more, Moses always taunts the animals with stories of Sugarcandy Mountain, a mythical place filled with food and leisure where animals go after they die.

Major is a twelve-year-old Middle White boar. He is venerated and respected for his years and wisdom by the other animals. Old Major introduces the idea of revolution to the animals and teaches them the song, *Beasts of England*, that will become their anthem. His ideals of a new world order where animals rule and respect themselves are noble ones, but unfortunately short lived on Animal Farm.

Boxer and Clover are two cart horses who do most of the heavy work on the farm. They are not very bright. As a consequence, Napoleon can rely on their blind faith. Boxer, in particular, is known for saying, "If Comrade Napoleon said it, then it must be right." Because of this unquestioning allegiance, Boxer literally works himself to death.

Mollie, the spoiled mare, has difficulty embracing the new life-style after the Rebellion. There are no ribbons for her mane or sugar for her sweet tooth in the new order. Mollie does not last long on Animal Farm; instead, she seeks out new lodgings at a neighboring farm where she may enjoy the good life once again.

Benjamin, an old mule, keeps as much to himself after the Rebellion as before. His independent stance permits him to see events more clearly than the other animals. He is known to be grumpy most of the time, but he can also offer cynical yet realistic commentary on the situation at hand.

Snowball, with Napoleon, is one of two pigs who take over the direction of the farm after the Rebellion. He is known to be an eloquent speaker. Further, he can envision long-term good for the farm resulting from innovative changes to its operation. Napoleon, his main adversary, works against these improvement ideas. Eventually, the rivalry results in Snowball's expulsion from the farm. From that point on, Snowball is used as a foil to explain away any mishap or failure on the farm.

Napoleon is the only Berkshire Boar on the Farm and therefore is marked differently from the other pigs. Napoleon has visions of grandeur—his own, that is. Though he does not display the leadership qualities that Snowball possesses, Napoleon is skillful at undermining any idea that is not his own. Then, he turns this same idea into a plan of his own device and to his own benefit. Napoleon is the consummate powermonger, who, not unsurprisingly, becomes a reinvention of Mr. Jones.

Squealer, a small pig, acts as mouthpiece, public relations man, and interpreter of the ever-changing truth for the powers-that-be. Of the three principal pigs (Snowball, Napoleon, Squealer), he stands out as the one most handy with words, such that it has been said that when Squealer speaks he can turn black into white. ✤

Critical Views

GRAHAM GREENE ON THE SADNESS OF *ANIMAL FARM*

[Graham Greene (1904–1991), aside from being one of the most significant British novelists of the twentieth century, was a prolific book reviewer for the *Spectator* and other periodicals. In this review of *Animal Farm*, Greene, noting the tale's political satire, remarks on its sadness as an account of the tribulations of hard-working animals.]

It is a welcome sign of peace that Mr George Orwell is able to publish his 'fairy story' *Animal Farm*, a satire upon the totalitarian state and one state in particular. I have heard a rumour that the manuscript was at one time submitted to the Ministry of Information, that huge cenotaph of appeasement, and an official there took a poor view of it. 'Couldn't you make them some other animal,' he is reported as saying in reference to the dictator and his colleagues, 'and not pigs?'

For this is the story of a political experiment on a farm where the animals, under the advice of a patriarchal porker, get organised and eventually drive out Mr Jones, the human owner. ⟨. . .⟩

It is a sad fable, and it is an indication of Mr Orwell's fine talent that it is really sad—not a mere echo of human failings at one remove. We do become involved in the fate of Molly the Cow, old Benjamin the Donkey, and Boxer the poor devil of a hard-working, easily deceived Horse. Snowball is driven out by Napoleon, who imposes his solitary leadership with the help of a gang of savage dogs, and slowly the Seven Commandments become altered or erased, until at last on the barn door appears only one sentence. 'All animals are equal, but some animals are more equal than others.'

If Mr Walt Disney is looking for a real subject, here it is: it has all the necessary humour, and it has, too, the subdued lyrical quality he can sometimes express so well. But is it perhaps a little too real for him?

—Graham Greene, [Review of *Animal Farm*], *Evening Standard* (London), 10 August 1945, p. 6

KINGSLEY-MARTIN ON ORWELL'S SATIRE OF THE SOVIET UNION

[Kingsley Martin (1879–1969) was a significant British historian and critic. Among his books are *Fascism, Democracy and the Press* (1938), *The Rise of French Liberal Thought* (1954), and *Britain in the Sixties* (1963). He was also a longtime editor of the left-leaning periodical, the *New Statesman*. In this review, Martin comments on Orwell's satire of the Soviet Union but believes that it is superficial and misleading.]

Mr Orwell's Devils have been numerous and, since he is a man of integrity, he chooses real evils to attack. His latest satire, beautifully written, amusing and, if you don't take it too seriously, a fair corrective of much silly worship of the Soviet Union, suggests to me that he is reaching the exhaustion of idealism and approaching the bathos of cynicism. ⟨. . .⟩

There is plenty in the U.S.S.R. to satirise, and Mr Orwell does it well. How deftly the fairy story of the animals who, in anticipation of freedom and plenty, revolt against the tyrannical farmer, turns into a rollicking caricature of the Russian Revolution! His shafts strike home. We all know of the sheep, who drown discussion by the bleating of slogans; we have all noticed, with a wry smile, the gradual change of Soviet doctrine under the pretence that it is no change and then that the original doctrine was an anti-Marxist error. (The best thing in Mr Orwell's story is the picture of the puzzled animals examining the Original Principles of the Revolution, and finding them altered: 'All animals are equal,' said the slogan; to which is added, 'but some are more equal than others.') The falsehoods about Trotsky, whose part in the revolutionary period, only secondary to Lenin's, has been gradually erased from the Soviet history books, is another fair count against Stalinite methods. The story of the loyal horse who worked until his lungs burst and was finally sent off to the knackers' yard is told with a genuine pathos; it represents a true and hateful aspect of every revolutionary struggle. Best of all is the character of the donkey who says little, but is always sure that the more things change the more they will be the same, that men will always be oppressed and exploited whether they have revolutions and high ideals or not.

⟨. . .⟩ In short, if we read the satire as a gibe at the failings of the U.S.S.R. and realise that it is historically false and neglectful of the complex truth about Russia, we shall enjoy it and be grateful for our laugh. But which will Mr Orwell do next? Having fired his bolt against Stalin, he could return to the attack on British or American Capitalism as seen through the eyes say, of an Indian peasant; the picture would be about as true or as false. Alternatively, there is the Church of Rome, Yogi, or at a pinch, the more tedious effort to help find the solution of any of the problems that actually face Stalin, Mr Attlee, Mr Orwell and the rest of us.
—Kingsley Martin, "Soviet Satire," *New Statesman and Nation,* 8 September 1945, pp. 165–66

ARTHUR M. SCHLESINGER, JR., ON THE UNIVERSALITY OF *ANIMAL FARM*

[Arthur M. Schlesinger, jr. (b. 1927) is one of the most important American historians of our time. Among his many books are *The Age of Jackson* (1945) and *The Age of Roosevelt* (1957–60). In this review, Schlesinger notes that *Animal Farm* goes well beyond being merely a satire of Soviet Russia, but that a knowledge of conditions in the Soviet Union will lend an added resonance to the book.]

A simple story perhaps, but a story of deadly simplicity. In *Animal Farm* Orwell handles the perplexities which Silone and Koestler have faced in terms of the psychological novel by means of superbly controlled and brilliantly sustained satire. He writes absolutely without coyness or whimsicality and with such gravity and charm that *Animal Farm* becomes an independent creation, standing quite apart from the object of its comment. The qualities of pathos in the tale of the betrayal of the animals—in the account, for example, of Boxer, the faithful horse—would compel the attention of persons who never heard of the Russian Revolution.

But appreciation of the precision and bite of the satire increases with knowledge of events in Russia. The steadiness and lucidity of Orwell's merciless wit are reminiscent of Anatole France and even of Swift. The exact and deadpan transposition of struggle between Stalin and Trotsky, the fight over industrialization, the Moscow trials, the diplomatic shenanigans with Britain and Germany, the NKVD, the resurrection of the state church, and so on, will be a continuing delight to any one familiar with recent Soviet developments. The story should be read in particular by liberals who still cannot understand how Soviet performance has fallen so far behind Communist professions. *Animal Farm* is a wise, compassionate and illuminating fable for our times.

—Arthur M. Schlesinger, jr., "Mr. Orwell and the Communists," *New York Times Book Review*, 25 August 1946, pp. 1, 28

EDMUND WILSON ON THE EXCELLENCE OF *ANIMAL FARM*

[Edmund Wilson (1895–1972) was perhaps the leading American literary critic of his age. Among his many works are *Axel's Castle: A Study in the Imaginative Literature of 1870–1930* (1931), *The Wound and the Bow* (1947), and *Patriotic Gore* (1962). In this review, Wilson finds the satire and wit of *Animal Farm* to be worthy of Swift and Voltaire.]

Animal Farm, by George Orwell, is a satirical animal fable about the progress—or backsliding—of the Russian Revolution. If you are told that the story deals with a group of cows, horses, pigs, sheep, and poultry which decide to expel their master and run his farm for themselves but eventually turn into something almost indistinguishable from human beings, with the pigs as a superior caste exploiting the other animals very much as the farmer did, and if you hear that Stalin figures as a pig named Napoleon and Trotsky as a pig named Snowball, you may not think it sounds particularly promising. But the truth is that it is absolutely first-rate. As a rule, I have difficulty in swallowing these modern animal fables; I can't bear Kipling's stories about the horses that resist trade-unionism and the beehive that is ruined by Socialism, nor have I ever been able to come under the spell of *The Wind in the Willows.* But Mr Orwell has worked out his theme with a simplicity, a wit, and a dryness that are closer to La Fontaine and Gay, and has written in a prose so plain and spare, so admirably proportioned to his purpose, that *Animal Farm* even seems very creditable if we compare it with Voltaire and Swift.

—Edmund Wilson, [Review of *Animal Farm*], *New Yorker*, 7 September 1946, p. 97

NORTHROP FRYE ON THE FAILINGS OF *ANIMAL FARM*

[Northrop Frye (1912–1991) was one of the leading critics of the century and author of many works, including *Fearful Symmetry: A Study of William Blake* (1947), *Anatomy of Criticism* (1957), and *The Great Code: The Bible and Literature* (1982). For many years he was University Professor and Chancellor at Victoria University in Toronto. In this review, Frye finds many deficiencies in *Animal Farm* both in execution and in its political message.]

George Orwell's satire on Russian Communism, *Animal Farm*, has just appeared in America, but its fame has preceded it, and surely by now everyone has heard of the fable of the animals who revolted and set up a republic on a farm, how the pigs seized control and how, led by a dictatorial boar named Napoleon, they finally became human beings walking on two legs and carrying whips just as the old Farmer Jones had done. ⟨. . .⟩

The story is very well-written, especially the Snowball episode, which suggests that the Communist 'Trotskyite' is a conception on much the same mental plane as the Nazi 'Jew,' and the vicious irony of the end of Boxer the work horse is perhaps really great satire. On the other hand, the satire on the episode corresponding to the German invasion seems to me both silly and heartless, and the final metamorphosis of pigs into humans at the end is a fantastic disruption of the sober logic of the tale. The reason for the change in method was to conclude the story by showing the end of Communism under Stalin as a replica of its beginning under the Czar. Such an alignment is, of course, complete nonsense, and as Mr Orwell must know it to be nonsense, his motive for adopting it was presumably that he did not know how otherwise to get his allegory rounded off with a neat epigrammatic finish. ⟨. . .⟩

A really searching satire on Russian Communism, then, would be more deeply concerned with the underlying reasons for its transformation from a proletarian dictatorship into a kind of parody of the Catholic Church. Mr Orwell does not bother with motivation: he makes his Napoleon inscrutably ambitious, and lets it go at that, and as far as he is concerned some old reactionary bromide like 'you can't change human nature' is as good a moral as any other for his fable.

—Northrop Frye, "Turning New Leaves," *Canadian Forum* No. 311 (December 1946): 211–12

GEORGE ORWELL ON THE INSPIRATION FOR *ANIMAL FARM*

[In a preface written for a 1947 edition of *Animal Farm*, George Orwell explains how he came to write his tale, and he also elucidates some of the political satire imbedded in it.]

On my return from Spain I thought of exposing the Soviet myth in a story that could be easily understood by almost anyone and which could be easily translated into other languages. However the actual details of the story did not come to me for some time until one day (I was then living in a small village) I saw a little boy, perhaps ten years old, driving a huge cart-horse along a narrow path, whipping it whenever it tried to turn. It struck me that if only such animals became aware of their strength we should have no power over them, and that men exploit animals in much the same way as the rich exploit the proletariat.

I proceeded to analyse Marx's theory from the animals' point of view. To them it was clear that the concept of a class struggle between humans was pure illusion, since whenever it was necessary to exploit animals, all humans united against them: the true struggle is between animals and humans. From this point of departure, it was not difficult to elaborate the story. I did not write it out till 1943, for I was always engaged on other work which gave me no time; and in the end, I included some events, for example the Teheran Conference, which were taking place while I was writing. Thus the main outlines of the story were in my mind over a period of six years before it was actually written.

I do not wish to comment on the work; if it does not speak for itself, it is a failure. But I should like to emphasise two points: first, that although the various episodes are taken from the actual history of the Russian Revolution, they are dealt with schematically and their chronological order is changed; this was necessary for the symmetry of the story. The second point has been missed by most critics, possibly because I did not emphasise it sufficiently. A number of readers may finish the book with the impression that it ends in the complete reconciliation of the pigs and the humans. That was not my intention; on the contrary I meant it to end on a loud note of discord, for I wrote it immediately after the Teheran Conference which everybody thought had established the best possible relations between the USSR and the West. I personally did not believe that such good relations would last long; and, as events have shown, I wasn't far wrong. . . .

—George Orwell, "Preface to *Animal Farm*" (1947), *Collected Essays, Journalism and Letters,* ed. Sonia Orwell and Ian Angus (New York: Harcourt, Brace & World, 1968), Vol. 3, pp. 405–6

♣

[Bertrand Russell (1872–1970), one of the leading British philosophers of the twentieth century, was also a prolific political commentator. Among his works on politics and society are *Power: A New Social Analysis* (1938), *Human Society in Ethics and Politics* (1954), and *Common Sense and Nuclear Warfare* (1959). In this extract, Russell believes that *Animal Farm* is a product of Orwell's despair over the state of politics, but that, unlike Swift's, his satire is always leavened by kindliness.]

Orwell was not by nature pessimistic or unduly obsessed by politics. He had wide interests, and would have been genial if he had lived at a less painful time. In an admirable essay on Dickens, he even allows himself to comment not unsympathetically upon Dickens's belief that all would be well if people would behave well, and that it is not the reform of institutions that is really important. Orwell had too much human sympathy to imprison himself in a creed. He sums up Dickens by describing him as 'laughing, with a touch of anger in his laughter, but no triumph, no malignity. It is the face of a man who is always fighting against something, but who fights in the open and is not frightened, the face of a man who is *generously angry*—in other words, of a nineteenth-century liberal, a free intelligence, a type hated with equal hatred by all the smelly little orthodoxies which are now contending for our souls.'

But our age is dominated by politics, as the fourth century was dominated by theology, and it is by his political writings that Orwell will be remembered—especially by *Animal Farm*.

Animal Farm naturally suggests comparison with *Gulliver's Travels*, particularly with the part dealing with the Houyhnhnms. Orwell's animals, it is true, including even the noble horse, are not much like Swift's incarnations of frosty reason. But Orwell, like Swift after Queen Anne's death, belonged to a beaten party, and both men travelled through defeat to despair. Both embodied their despair in biting and masterly satire. But while Swift's satire expresses universal and indiscriminating hate, Orwell's has always an undercurrent of kindliness: he hates the enemies of those whom he loves, whereas Swift could only love (and that faintly) the enemies of those whom he hated. Swift's misanthropy, moreover, sprang mainly from thwarted ambition, while Orwell's sprang from the betrayal of generous ideals by their nominal advocates. In a penetrating essay on 'Gulliver', Orwell set forth justly and convincingly the pettiness of Swift's hopes and the stupidity of his ideals. In neither respect did Orwell share Swift's defeats.

—Bertrand Russell, "George Orwell," *World Review* No. 16 (June 1950): 5–6

CHRISTOPHER HOLLIS ON THE TECHNIQUE OF WRITING ANIMAL FABLES

[Christopher Hollis (1902–1977) was a British historian and critic and a chairman of the board of the publishing company Hollis & Carter. He is the author of *The American Heresy* (1930), *Dryden* (1933), and *History of Britain in Modern Times* (1946). In this extract from his study of Orwell, Hollis discusses the principles of writing animal fables—they must be simple, whimsical, and light-hearted—and gauges how well Orwell accomplished his purpose in *Animal Farm*.]

The interpretation of the fable is plain enough. Major, Napoleon, Snowball—Lenin, Stalin and Trotzky—Pilkington and Frederick, the two groups of non-Communist powers—the Marxian thesis, as expounded by Major, that society is divided into exploiters and exploited and that all the exploited need to do is to rise up, to expel the exploiters and seize the 'surplus value' which the exploiters have previously annexed to themselves—the Actonian thesis that power corrupts and the Burnhamian thesis that the leaders of the exploited, having used the rhetoric of equality to get rid of the old exploiters, establish in their place not a classless society but themselves as a new governing class—the greed and unprincipled opportunism of the non-Communist states, which are ready enough to overthrow the Communists by force so long as they imagine that their overthrow will be easy but begin to talk of peace when they find the task difficult and when they think that they can use the Communists to satisfy their greed—the dishonour among total thugs, as a result of which, though greed may make original ideology irrelevant, turning pigs into men and men into pigs, the thugs fall out among themselves, as the Nazis and the Communists fell out, not through difference of ideology but because in a society of utter baseness and insincerity there is no motive of confidence. The interpretation is so plain that no serious critic can dispute it. Those Russian critics who have professed to see in it merely a general satire on bureaucracy without any special reference to any particular country can hardly be taken seriously.

Yet even a total acceptance of Orwell's political opinions would not in itself make *Animal Farm* a great work of art. The world is full of animal fables in which this or that country is symbolized by this or that animal, and very tedious affairs the greater number of them are—and that, irrespective of whether we agree or disagree with their opinions. To be a great book, a book of animal fables requires literary greatness as well as a good cause. Such greatness *Animal Farm* surely possesses. As Orwell fairly claimed, *Animal Farm* 'was the first book in which I tried, with full consciousness of what I was doing, to fuse political purpose and artistic purpose into one whole'—and he succeeded.

The problems that are set by this peculiar form of art, which makes animals behave like human beings, are clear. The writer must throughout be successful in preserving a delicate and whimsical balance. As Johnson truly says in his criticism of Dryden's *Hind and the Panther,* there is an initial absurdity in making animals discuss complicated intellectual problems—the nature of the Church's authority in Dryden's case, the communist ideology in Orwell's. The absurdity can only be saved from ridicule if the author is able to couch his argument in very simple terms and to draw his illustrations from the facts of animal life. In this Orwell is as successful as he could be—a great deal more successful incidentally than Dryden, who in the excitement of the argument often forgets that it is animals who are supposed to be putting it forward. The practical difficulties of the conceit must either be ignored or apparently solved in some simple and striking—if possible, amusing—fashion. Since obviously they could not in reality be solved at all, the author merely makes himself ridiculous if he allows himself to get bogged down in tedious and detailed explanations which at the end of all cannot in the nature of things explain anything. Thus Orwell is quite right merely to ignore the difficulties of language, to assume that the animals can communicate with one another by speech—or to assume that the new ordinance which forbids any animal to take another animal's life could be applied with only the comparatively mild consequence of gradual increase in animal population. He is justified in telling us the stories of the two attacks by men for the recapture of the Farm but in refusing to spoil his story by allowing the men to take the full measures which obviously men would take if they found themselves in such an impossible situation. The means by which the animals rout the men are inevitably signally unconvincing if we are to consider them seriously at all. It would as obviously be ridiculous to delay for pages to describe how animals build windmills or how they write up commandments on a wall. It heightens the comedy to give a passing sentence of description to their hauling the stone up a hill so that it may be broken into manageable fractions when it falls over the precipice, or to Squealer, climbing a ladder to paint up his message.

The animal fable, if it is to succeed at all, ought clearly to carry with it a gay and light-hearted message. It must be full of comedy and laughter. The form is too far removed from reality to tolerate sustained bitterness. Both Chaucer and La Fontaine discovered this in their times, and the trouble with Orwell was that the lesson which he wished to teach was not ultimately a gay lesson. It was not the lesson that mankind had its foibles and its follies but that all would be well in the end. It was more nearly a lesson of despair—the lesson that anarchy was intolerable, that mankind could not be ruled without entrusting power somewhere or other and, to whomsoever power was entrusted, it was almost certain to be abused. For power was itself corrupting. But it was Orwell's twisted triumph that in the relief of the months immediately after the war mankind was probably not prepared to take such dark medicine if it had been offered to it undiluted. It accepted it because it came in this gay and coloured and fanciful form.

—Christopher Hollis, *A Study of George Orwell* (Chicago: Regnery, 1956), pp. 145–47

RICHARD REES ON ORWELL'S TEMPERAMENT

[Richard Rees (1900–1970) was a prolific British author, editor, and translator. He wrote *Brave Men: A Study of D. H. Lawrence and Simone Weil* (1958), *A Theory of My Time* (1963), and *George Orwell: Fugitive from the Camp of Victory* (1961), from which the following extract is taken. Here, Rees studies Orwell's temperament when writing *Animal Farm,* believing that Orwell had renounced the sense of optimism in regard to political and social change that had characterized his earlier work.]

Animal Farm is so well known that it cannot be necessary to do more than mention some of its major felicities: the friendship between the noble, dimwitted cart horse Boxer and the resigned, cynical and clear-headed donkey Benjamin; the incorrigible behavior of Mollie, the white mare who used to draw Mr. Jones' trap (when the animals first explore the farmhouse she is discovered admiring herself in a mirror "in a very foolish manner," and later she deserts to the enemy, having been lured away, by a man, with presents of sugar and red ribbon); and the perfidy of Napoleon, who sells Boxer to a Slaughterer and Glue Boiler when his strength has given out after years of Herculean labor for the farm.

The immediate, terrific impact of *Animal Farm* was perhaps partly due to the fact that the high tide of Russian popularity in England after Stalingrad was already ebbing in 1945, when the book was published. But it had in fact been almost completed by 1943, when Orwell was one of the very few whose experience and knowledge prevented them from indulging in rosy hopes of future sympathy and understanding between Russia and the West.

The air of blitheness and buoyancy which fills *Animal Farm,* as it does *Homage to Catalonia,* in spite of the depressing theme, suggests that Orwell was still comparatively optimistic when he wrote it. But by comparing the working class to animals, even noble and attractive ones, he implies that they are at an irremediable disadvantage in the class struggle. The animals' difficulty in using tools is emphasized several times in the book; and it is only the clever but repulsive and odious pigs who are able to learn to use a pen, walk on two legs, and pass themselves off as human beings. One is reminded of Orwell's attitude many years earlier, when he returned from Burma at the age of twenty-four:

> At that time failure seemed to me the only virtue. Every suspicion of self-advancement, even to "succeed" in life to the extent of earning a few hundreds a year, seemed to me spiritually ugly, a species of bullying.

It will be remembered that *Keep the Aspidistra Flying* was about a young man who held a sort of immature and self-centered version of the above doctrine; and although Orwell himself, having once found a political purpose for his writing, never relapsed into the mood of that early novel, it does appear in *Animal Farm,* and still more in *1984,* that he ceased to rely upon the generous, humane and unambitious instincts— the "crystal spirit"—of the common man as an effective political ally in the struggle against spiritual ugliness and bullying.
> —Richard Rees, *George Orwell: Fugitive from the Camp of Victory* (Carbondale: Southern Illinois University Press, 1961), pp. 85–86

STEPHEN JAY GREENBLATT ON ORWELL'S SATIRE ON THE WEST

[Stephen Jay Greenblatt (b. 1943), a professor of English at the University of California, is a leading literary critic and theorist and the author of *Renaissance Self-Fashioning* (1980), *Shakespearean Negotiations* (1988), *Learning to Curse: Essays in Early Modern Culture* (1990), and other works. In this extract, taken from a monograph written when he was an undergraduate, Greenblatt points out that Orwell's satire in *Animal Farm* is directed at Western capitalism as well as Soviet communism.]

The interpretation of *Animal Farm* in terms of Soviet history (Major, Napoleon, Snowball represent Lenin, Stalin, Trotsky) has been made many times and shall not be pursued further here. It is amusing, however, that many of the Western critics who astutely observe the barbs aimed at Russia fail completely to grasp Orwell's judgment of the West. After all, the pigs do not turn into alien monsters; they come to resemble those bitter rivals Mr. Pilkington and Mr. Frederick, who represent the Nazis and the Capitalists. All three major "powers" are despicable tyrannies, and the failure of the revolution is not seen in terms of ideology at all, but as a realization of Lord Acton's thesis, "Power tends to corrupt; absolute power corrupts absolutely." The initial spark of a revolution, the original intention of a constitution may have been an ideal of the good life, but the result is always the same—tyranny. Communism is no more or less evil than Fascism or Capitalism—they are all illusions which are inevitably used by the pigs as a means of satisfying their greed and their lust for power. Religion, too, is merely a toy of the oppressors and a device to divert the minds of the sufferers. Moses, the tame raven who is always croaking about the sweet, eternal life in Sugarcandy Mountain, flies after the deposed Farmer Jones, only to return when Napoleon has established his tyranny.

Animal Farm remains powerful satire even as the specific historical events it mocked recede into the past, because the book's major concern is not with these incidents but with the essential horror of the human condition. There have been, are, and always will be pigs in every society, Orwell states, and they will always grab power. Even more cruel is the conclusion that *everyone* in the society, wittingly or unwittingly, contributes to the pigs' tyranny. Boxer, the noblest (though not the wisest) animal on the farm, devotes his unceasing labor to the pigs, who, as has been noted, send him to the knacker when he has outlived his usefulness. There is real pathos as the sound of Boxer's hoofs drumming weakly on the back of the horse slaughterer's van grows fainter and dies away, and the reader senses that in that dying sound is the dying hope of humanity. But Orwell does not allow the mood of oppressive sadness to overwhelm the satire, and Squealer, "lifting his trotter and wiping away a tear," hastens to announce that, after receiving every attention a horse could have, Boxer died in his hospital bed, with the words "Napoleon is always right" on his withered lips. Frederick R. Karl, in *The Contemporary English Novel,* believes that *Animal Farm* fails as successful satire "by virtue of its predictability," but this terrifying predictability of the fate of all revolutions is just the point Orwell is trying to make. The grotesque end of the fable is not meant to shock the reader—indeed, chance and surprise are banished entirely from Orwell's world. The horror of both *Animal Farm* and the later *1984* is precisely the cold, orderly, predictable process by which decency, happiness, and hope are systematically and ruthlessly crushed.

—Stephen Jay Greenblatt, "George Orwell," *Three Modern Satirists: Waugh, Orwell, and Huxley* (New Haven: Yale University Press, 1965), pp. 64–66

GEORGE WOODCOCK ON *ANIMAL FARM* AS A POLITICAL PAMPHLET

[George Woodcock (b. 1912) is a leading Canadian critic and author. Among his many books are *The Canadians* (1979), *Strange Bedfellows: The State and the Arts in Canada* (1985), and *Oscar Wilde: The Double Image* (1989). In this extract from his book on Orwell, Woodcock notes that *Animal Farm* was written at a time when Orwell was interested in political pamphlets, and that in its simplicity and conciseness *Animal Farm* is itself a political pamphlet.]

"*Animal Farm*," said Orwell in 1947, "was the first book in which I tried, with full consciousness of what I was doing, to fuse political purpose and artistic purpose in one whole." He succeeded admirably, and produced a book so clear in intent and writing that the critic is usually rather nonplussed as to what he should say about it; all is so magnificently there, and the only thing that really needs to be done is to place this crystalline little book into its proper setting.

Conciseness of form and simplicity of language are the qualities which immediately strike one on opening *Animal Farm* after having read Orwell's earlier works of fiction. The fable is about a third the length of *Keep the Aspidistra Flying,* though the events of which it tells are much more complicated, and it is written in a bare English, uncluttered by metaphor, which contrasts strongly with both the elaborately literary diction of *Burmese Days* and the racy but sometimes over-rich narrative style of *Coming Up for Air.*

> Mr. Jones, of the Manor Farm, had locked the henhouses for the night, but was too drunk to remember to shut the popholes. With the ring of light from his lantern dancing from side to side, he lurched across the yard, kicked off his boots at the back door, drew himself a last glass of beer from the barrel in the scullery, and made his way up to bed, where Mrs. Jones was already snoring.

So it begins, and so it continues to the end, direct, exact and sharply concrete, letting events make their own impacts and stimulating the creation of mental pictures, so that one remembers the book as a series of lively visual images held together by a membrane of almost transparent prose.

There was no doubt in Orwell's mind about his intention in writing *Animal Farm.* He felt that the English in 1943 were allowing their admiration for the military heroism of the Russians to blind them to the faults of the Communist regime, and he also believed that the Communists were using their position as unofficial representatives of Russia in England to prevent the truth from being known, as they had done in Spain. *Animal Farm* was meant to set his compatriots thinking again.

At that time Orwell was fascinated by the craft of pamphleteering, which had something of a wartime vogue among British writers, so that not only likely people, such as Orwell, Read and Spender, produced pamphlets, but even unlikely people such as Forster, Eliot and Henry Miller. Besides the three unimpressive and not very successful pamphlets which he himself wrote in the 1940's, Orwell edited with Reginald Reynolds an anthology of classic pamphlets from the past, entitled *British Pamphleteers;* he believed that a revival of pamphleteering was possible and desirable. In a pamphlet one could state a case simply and concisely, and it would stand on its own feet as no article in a periodical could ever do. But pamphleteering in fact never took on that new lease of life in the postwar years which Orwell had anticipated; this was due partly to lack of interest among the booksellers and partly to the devitalization of British politics after 1945.

Yet *Animal Farm,* which was really a pamphlet in fictional form, did succeed, because it created within the dimension of a fable a perfect and self-consistent microcosm. There was nothing very original about the basic idea of a community of animals acting like men, which had been used about fifteen hundred years before by the anonymous Indian author of that extraordinary collection of political fables, the *Panchatantra.* But, like the authors of the *Panchatantra,* Orwell gave his work freshness by inducing that peculiar blend of humor, incongruity and apparent candor which creates in the reader a willingness to suspend disbelief and to transfer himself in mind into the changed dimensions of a world where the pursuits of men can be seen dispassionately because it is animals which are following them.

—George Woodcock, *The Crystal Spirit: A Study of George Orwell* (Boston: Little, Brown, 1966), pp. 192–94

[Jenni Calder (b. 1941) is Museum Editor at the National Museum of Scotland and the author of many works of criticism, including *Women and Marriage in Victorian Fiction* (1976), *RLS: A Life Study* (1980), and a study of *Animal Farm* and *Nineteen Eighty-four* (1987). In this extract, Calder studies Orwell's treatment of animals in *Animal Farm,* noting that, although they are allegories, they are nevertheless full-fledged characters.]

Animal Farm crystallises the ideas present in the Ukrainian edition's introduction into a plain, English and allegorical version of *Darkness At Noon.* V. S. Pritchett describes the book as "the traditional English fable" and there is certainly something almost homely about Orwell's treatment. He avoids the problem of digesting an experience that is second-hand. He attempts neither realism nor interpretation. He allows the facts, shaped and coloured by allegory, to speak for themselves. The satire too moves within the allegory, which uses the English countryside and farm beasts familiar to him. The allegorical method far from reducing what he has to say to the coldness of symbols gives the book a warmth and texture which Orwell rarely achieved. The animals are never mere representations. They have a breathing individuality that is lacking in most of Orwell's human characters. There are no barriers between Orwell and his understanding and affection for his characters, no reticence, no distracting complications, no sociological points to be made. Boxer, the cart horse, for instance, does not simply represent a Stakhanov figure. He is attractive in his own right, and the incident in which the pigs arrange for him to be taken to the glue factory is one of the most moving passages in the whole of Orwell's writing.

Nor is Orwell's handling of his animal characters sentimental. It is simple. Relationships are presented on their simplest levels. This makes the bewildered reaction to the pigs' power, the involvement of belief in political expedience, even more shattering. The absence of barriers in the method of characterisation can also be felt in the overwhelming logic of the story's development. The pigs' assumption of leadership after the initial revolt, the process of corruption gently underlined, the banishing of Snowball, the Trotsky figure—each incident melts into the overall development. There are no jerks, no sudden piling up of emphases, in the book's superbly controlled movement. The distortion of the original commandments and the animals' inability to challenge the leadership occur inevitably. Without venturing into analysis or explanation Orwell presents a compact and detailed statement of the corruption of revolution.

The allegory is very precise in its use of the major figures and incidents of the Russian Revolution. It expresses quite nakedly and with a complete lack of intellectual argument those aspects of Stalinism that most disturbed Orwell. At the same time the humbleness and warmth of the narrative give an attractive obliqueness without turning the direction of the satire. We can feel compassion for Orwell's creatures in a way that we cannot for Winston Smith, for the stark narrative of *Nineteen Eighty-Four* stuns our capacity for reaction. But *Animal Farm* is equally relentless in its message. The relentless quality is partly contained in the even tone of the language. In the midst of describing hardship and disaster it does not vary—it matches the pathetic doggedness of the animals themselves. In no other work does Orwell so successfully resist the temptation to launch into barely relevant side issues. The measured amalgam of straightforward vocabulary and colloquial phrase has a strange power, perhaps because Orwell writes with a complete lack of self-consciousness, as if he were describing recognised facts, and without the pretense of inserting himself into the animals' minds:

> Meanwhile life was hard. The winter was as cold as the last one had been, and food was even shorter. Once again all rations were reduced, except those of the pigs and the dogs. A too rigid equality in rations, Squealer explained, would have been contrary to the principles of Animalism. In any case he had no difficulty in proving to the other animals that they were *not* in reality short of food, whatever the appearances might be. . . . The animals believed every word of it. Truth to tell, Jones and all he stood for had almost faded out of their memories. They knew that life nowadays was harsh and bare, that they were often hungry and often cold, and that they were usually working

when they were not asleep. But doubtless it had been worse in the old days. They were glad to believe so. Besides, in those days they had been slaves and now they were free, and that made all the difference, as Squealer did not fail to point out.

Orwell identifies himself with the animals while maintaining his distance, in the same way as he identified himself with tramps or the unemployed. His sympathetic detachment reinforces the plain strength of the prose. The words are simple, the sentences short, many with only a single clause. The simplicity gives an authentic quality to the writing. As in so much of Orwell's writing he does not erect clusters of words and phrases which come between him and his reader and disguise meaning rather than illuminate it. Adjectives like "harsh and bare", "cold", "hungry" do all the work that is needed without embroidery, although they are the kind of adjectives that often become removed from their plain meanings.
—Jenni Calder, *Chronicles of Conscience: A Study of George Orwell and Arthur Koestler* (London: Secker & Warburg, 1968), pp. 224–26

ROBERT A. LEE ON THE CORRUPTION OF LANGUAGE IN *ANIMAL FARM*

[Robert A. Lee is the author of *Orwell's Fiction* (1969), from which the following extract is taken. Here, Lee observes that Orwell criticizes nearly all political systems in *Animal Farm* and concludes that the true message of the story is that human beings will submit to tyranny if they allow their language to be corrupted and taken away from their control.]

Power inevitably corrupts the best of intentions, apparently no matter who possesses the power: At the end, all the representatives of the various ideologies are indistinguishable—they are all pigs, all pigs are humans. Communism is no better and no worse than capitalism or fascism; the ideals of socialism were long ago lost in Clover's uncomprehending gaze over the farm.

Religion is merely a toy for the corrupters, neither offensive nor helpful to master or slave. But perhaps more distressing yet is the realization that everyone, the good and the bad, the deserving and the wicked, are not only contributors to the tyranny, are not only powerless before it, but are unable to understand it. Boxer thinks that whatever Napoleon says is right; Clover can only vaguely feel, and cannot communicate, that things are not exactly right; Benjamin thinks that it is in the nature of the world that things go wrong. The potential hope of the book is finally expressed only in terms of ignorance (Boxer), wistful inarticulateness (Clover), or the tired, cynical belief that things never change (Benjamin). The inhabitants of this world seem to deserve their fate.

One must finally ask, however, with all this despair and bleakness what are the actual bases for the tyranny of Animal Farm. Is the terrorism of the dogs the most crucial aspect? Is it this that rules the animals? Boxer's power is seen as superior to this violence and force. Is the basis of the tonal despair the pessimistic belief in the helplessness of the mass of the animals? Orwell elsewhere states again and again his faith in the common people. It seems to me that the basis of this society's evil is the inability of its inhabitants to ascertain truth and that this is demonstrated through the theme of the corruption of language. So long as the animals cannot remember the past, because it is continually altered, they have no control over the present and hence over the future. A society which cannot control its language is, says Orwell, doomed to be oppressed in terms which deny it the very most elemental aspects of humanity: To live in a world which allows the revised form of the seventh commandment of Animal Farm is not merely to renounce the belief in the possibility of human equality, but in the blatant perversion of language, the very concept of objective reality is lost.

The mode by which the recognition of reality is denied is the corruption of language. When a society no longer maintains its language as a common basis by which value, idea, and fact are to be exchanged, those who control the means of communication have the most awful of powers—they literally can create the truth they choose. Animal Farm, then, seems to be in one respect only an extension of *Burmese Days*—the common problem is the failure of communication and its corollary, community. But if in *Burmese Days* their failure was contingent, in *Animal Farm* it is brought about by willful manipulation.

—Robert A. Lee, *Orwell's Fiction* (Notre Dame, IN: University of Notre Dame Press, 1969), pp. 126–27

DAVID L. KUBAL ON NATURAL INSTINCTS IN HUMANS AND ANIMALS

[David L. Kubal (b. 1936), a former professor of English at California State University at Los Angeles, is the author of *The Consoling Intelligence: Responses to Literary Modernism* (1982) and *Outside the Whale* (1972), a study of Orwell from which the following extract is taken. Here, Kubal believes that the fundamental point of *Animal Farm* is that both human beings and animals possess natural instincts that are inherently valuable, but that these instincts can be easily corrupted by society.]

In *Animal Farm* Orwell illustrates—better than in any other work—both his affection for animals and his idea that certain civilizing influences threaten the moral dimension of the instincts; that "animals" may begin to resemble men until it is "impossible to say which [is] which." In light of this one can see that he makes use of the beast fable for two principal reasons: It provides a suitable vehicle for satire, and it is also thematically relevant. Animals are humorous in themselves, can serve as convenient metaphors for certain vices and virtues (pigs are greedy; donkeys, stubborn, and horses, hardworking, etc.), and finally, they can symbolize the positive, biological instincts. They are communal, loyal, and self-sacrificing. It is important to note in the satire that the animals' corruption results from contact with man or the tools of his civilization. Not until after they win the Battle of the Cowshed and fully assume Farmer Jones's place does injustice begin. The pigs, Snowball and Napoleon, weaken themselves by living in the farmhouse. And, importantly, the dogs, Bluebell, Jessie, and Pincher, are taken from their mother at birth and put through a form of brainwashing to turn them into brutal killers. Mollie, the foolish and vain mare, has been spoiled by Jones, and Moses, the conniving, clerical raven, has learned his theology from the outside world.

The point that Orwell makes here is not that the bare, natural instincts are politically or socially sufficient. As George Woodcock contends, nevertheless, he tended to believe, like the romantics, that man possessed inherent virtues which were the foundation for a moral life and which contemporary culture was bent on eliminating. This anarchistic aspect was, of course, present in his thought, but it should not be overemphasized. As I have continually stressed, he never asserted perfectibility inside, and certainly not outside, the social order; institutions, based on a conscious moral and historical sense, were required to give the person direction and order. Indeed, if in *Animal Farm* he symbolically suggests the ethical validity of the natural instincts, he also underlines how easily these instincts can be perverted. And if they are never totally obliterated—Benjamin, the donkey, survives on the periphery—they are, as in the proles, of little political value. In a situation like Animal Farm or Oceania, however, where almost every element of existence can be manipulated, if there is a hope it must lie in the uncontrollable, the nonrational. Here again Orwell's relationship with Lawrence as well as Forster is apparent. Although there are important differences in emphasis among them in this matter, all three felt that especially in a highly industrial and organized society the irrational and spontaneous elements in human character must be given play.

The artistic value of *Animal Farm*, then, rests on Orwell's choice of metaphor and form. The conflict between biological instinct and civilization is succinctly mirrored in the animals' revolution against Farmer Jones. The allegorical form itself suggests the universality of the drama. The historical relevance, the fact that the author was satirizing the Soviet revolution, is, as I suggested, of comparatively minor importance. It cannot be overlooked, certainly, since it gives his major theme a definite historical validity. Even though *Animal Farm* remains as the only completely successful example of his combining of aesthetic and political intentions, it should not be assumed that it is a "sport" in his work.

> —David L. Kubal, *Outside the Whale: George Orwell's Art and Politics* (Notre Dame, IN: University of Notre Dame Press, 1972), pp. 125–27

❖

T. R. Fyvel on *Animal Farm* as a Children's Book

[T. R. Fyvel is the pseudonym of Raphael Joseph Feiwel (1907–1985), the founder of the intellectual journal *Encounter* and a longtime editor of the *Jewish Chronicle.* In this extract from his memoir of Orwell, Fyvel remembers how Orwell was dismayed that *Animal Farm* was placed in the children's section of bookstores.]

However interesting the essays, Orwell's prestige rests in the end on *Animal Farm* and *Nineteen Eighty-Four,* and as I read the two books again I was struck by their contrast. *Animal Farm,* which he wrote in 1943–4, when reasonably happily married and with Eileen an appreciative listener as he worked on it, seems a sunny tale of the countryside. By contrast, *Nineteen Eighty-Four,* which he wrote four years later when struggling against illness on Jura, is all inferno, a story of permanent metropolitan darkness.

To be sure, *Animal Farm* is also a story of frustration and cruelty. From the first page onwards, the revolt of the domestic animals of which it tells is predestined to fail. The final scene . when the bewildered animals look from their ruling pigs to the neighbouring men and cannot tell which is which, is already inherent in the opening where the old boar Major talks of a glorious revolutionary animal Utopia to come. But the events in between, as they gently unroll on Animal Farm, seem bathed in a permanent, benign sunshine. I remember how when I remarked on it, Orwell half admitted that he loved his farm whose workings and seasons he painted in such precise detail.

This loving detail was one reason for the astonishing success of the little allegory. There are others.

One can see that for adult readers there was the relentless fairy-tale logic of his satire on the course of the Soviet revolution. Orwell had turned over *Animal Farm* in his mind for a long time, but I recall his saying that what triggered him was the wartime Teheran Conference of 1943, where before the photographers, Churchill and Roosevelt smiled upon their monstrous tyrannical ally Stalin, who fought at their side against their monstrous enemy, Hitler. He also thought that the time when Western readers looked upon Stalin's tyranny through rose-coloured spectacles was most suitable for his attack upon it. He was not the first to suggest that in revolutions, the talk of democracy, liberty and the classless society was as a rule a cover for the ambitions of a new class elbowing its way to power, but the simplified fairy-tale form in which he presented this thesis was a touch of genius—it made the conclusion seem inevitable.

Even as read today, all the elements of the political satire fit perfectly. The animals, who after the overthrow of Farmer Jones sing revolutionary hymns as they parade on Sundays, still represent the first, brief libertarian enthusiasm of the Soviet revolutionaries, even if this far-off phase, so soon doomed, is today hardly remembered. The inscrutable boar Napoleon with his fierce dogs is still Stalin to the life. The boar Snowball, too clever by half, is still like the expelled Trotsky, whose political testament still has its followers. The building of the windmill, twice destroyed by human invaders, still resembles the once so hopefully publicized fulfilment of the Soviet Five Year Plans, as the animals toil for their new masters, the pigs.

But if on today's reading, *Animal Farm* is still a most convincing political satire, one can also see why it survives even more as the supreme modern intellectual fairy tale for children. Oddly, it was not Orwell's intention to provide children's reading. Remembering the incident from her housekeeper days in 1945, Susan Watson told me that after the successful publication, Orwell spent a full day rushing from bookshop to bookshop, asking for *Animal Farm* to be moved from the shelves of children's books where he often found it automatically placed.

Ultimately of course in vain. So successfully had he thought himself into the age-old European folk tradition of talking animals, that for children who read him he turned the domestic animals on the farm into immediately recognizable and memorable and sometimes lovable characters. Lovable above all was Boxer, the great cart-horse, poor in intellect but large in muscle, who could only say 'Comrade Napoleon is always right' and 'I must work harder.' With Boxer, as a child's favourite there is Clover, the gentle, maternal mare; there is the cynical old donkey Benjamin who observes everything with detachment (Koestler told me that during Orwell's Christmas visit to them in 1945, he and his wife called him 'Benjamin'). There are the savage dogs, the recognizably silly sheep—it is the believability of these characters which has turned *Animal Farm*, like *Gulliver's Travels*, into favoured children's reading: perhaps this is the fate of all the best satires.

—T. R. Fyvel, *George Orwell: A Personal Memoir* (New York: Macmillan, 1982), pp. 193–95

Daphne Patai on *Animal Farm* as a Feminist Critique of Socialism

[Daphne Patai (b. 1943) is a professor in the women's studies program and the department of Spanish and Portuguese at the University of Massachusetts at Amherst. She has written several books on Brazilian writers as well as *The Orwell Mystique: A Study in Male Ideology* (1984), from which the following extract is taken. Here, Patai reads *Animal Farm* as a feminist critique of socialism, although she admits that Orwell probably did not intend such a reading.]

With astonishing ease and aptness, *Animal Farm* can be read as a feminist critique of socialist revolutions which, through their failure to challenge patriarchy, have reproduced patriarchal values in the postrevolutionary period. In this reading of the fable, the pigs would be the sole male animals, while most of the other animals are stereotyped females: compliant, hardworking drones brainwashed with the illusion that their work is done for themselves, surrendering the fruits of their productive and reproductive labor to their masters, who tell them that there never was hope of a different future.

As in the power relations between men and women, so in *Animal Farm* "science" is used to explain that pigs need better and bigger rations because they are "brain workers," an argument offering the additional message that the dependent animals could not manage on their own. These brainworkers take on the "hard" work of supervising the political and economic life of the farm, consigning the rest to the "less important" tasks of physical labor and maintenance of the farm/home. By also assuming the burden of "international" relations (with neighboring farms), the pigs keep the others pure from any contaminating contact with the outside world—again, an uncanny parallel to the public/private split of ordinary patriarchal society. Whether the individual nonpig animal is big and strong like Boxer or small and weak like the hens, it is held in check by an ideology of its own ignorance and dependence, subjected to violence and intimidation, and urged to sacrifice itself. Such an animal is not likely to rebel. But, as Orwell himself pointed out, the book does not end on a totally pessimistic note. For in the recognition that pigs and men are identical lies the spark of knowledge that can lead to liberatory action.

It would be absurd, of course, to suggest that Orwell intended such a feminist reading of his text. Everything he ever wrote shows that he took the patriarchal family to be the proper model of society. In "The Lion and the Unicorn" he complained only that England was like "a family with the wrong members in control,"

> a rather stuffy Victorian family, with not many black sheep in it but with all its cupboards bursting with skeletons. It has rich relations who have to be kow-towed to and poor relations who are horribly sat upon, and there is a deep conspiracy of silence about the source of the family income. It is a family in which the young are generally thwarted and most of the power is in the hands of irresponsible uncles and bedridden aunts. Still, it is a

family. It has its private language and its common memories, and at the approach of an enemy it closes its ranks.

Of course, Orwell's version of just who is in control itself indicates his habitual misreading of the status of women in his own society. It seems to me that Orwell's complaint was on behalf of the brothers alone, as evidenced by his lack of awareness of the real disunity inherent in the patriarchal family.

It is fascinating to see Orwell describe the betrayal of the animals' revolution in terms so suggestive of women's experience under patriarchy. It is women who, more than any other group and regardless of the race and class to which they belong, have had their history obliterated, their words suppressed and forgotten, their position in society confounded by the doublethink of "All men are created equal," their legal rights denied, their labor in the home and outside of it expropriated and controlled by men, their reproductive capacities used against them, their desire for knowledge thwarted, their strivings turned into dependence—all of these under the single pretext that they are not "by nature" equipped to do the valued work of society, defined as what men do. When read as a feminist fable, however, *Animal Farm* has another important message. The origins of the Seven Commandments of Animalism lie in Major's warnings against adopting Man's ways: "And remember also that in fighting against Man, we must not come to resemble him. Even when you have conquered him, do not adopt his vices."

—Daphne Patai, *The Orwell Mystique: A Study in Male Ideology* (Amherst: University of Massachusetts Press, 1984), pp. 216–17

ALOK RAI ON THE REVOLUTION BETRAYED

[Alok Rai is the author of *Orwell and the Politics of Despair* (1988), from which the following extract is taken. Here, Rai sees *Animal Farm* as more than a satire on the Russian Revolution: the tale can be read as a nostalgic parable of the betrayal of the revolutionary spirit in general.]

In 1954 a critic suggested that *Animal Farm* was not really about the Russian Revolution but rather about the English 'revolution' which had seemed imminent in *The Lion and the Unicorn*. At a superficial level, this is clearly wrong. The tragic course of the Russian Revolution was very much in Orwell's mind in *Animal Farm,* to the extent that he made a correction, at proof stage, in recognition of Stalin's bravery, in the face of the German advance on Moscow: when the windmill was blown up, 'all the animals except Napoleon,' he insisted, 'flung themselves on their faces.' In an unpublished letter to his agent, now in the Berg collection in New York, Orwell wrote: 'If they question you again, please say that *Animal Farm* is intended as a satire on dictatorship in general but *of course* the Russian Revolution is the chief target. It is humbug to pretend anything else.' However, at a deeper level, it is still possible to see that the disappointment of his wartime hopes—his feeling that 'the political advance we seemed to make in 1940 has been gradually filched away from us'—lent its specific accent of anguish and despair to Orwell's critique of the Russian Revolution. In this mood, the grotesque transformation of the Russian Revolution, of which Orwell had been openly critical for some time, became a paradigmatic instance of *all* attempts at revolutionary social transformation.

One unintended effect of Orwell's avowedly leftist critique of the violence and tyranny of the pigs—the post-revolutionary elite—is that the regime of Jones, softened by nostalgia, begins to appear almost prelapsarian. This was *not* an avowal that Orwell could make explicitly. Thus, as the pigs become more ruthless and tyrannical they become, Orwell insists, more like men—like Pilkington and Frederick, like Jones. However, between the men who act like pigs and the pigs who become like men, there is precious little room for the animals who dreamt of revolution—or for the imagination that dreamt that dream. Thus, it is precisely my argument that with his wartime affirmation, the infectious euphoria that ended in disappointment, Orwell has boxed himself in. In this state, Orwell's intended allegory of the spontaneous revolution becomes an allegory of the revolution endlessly betrayed, a perverse and

brilliant distillation of the worst features of the Russian Revolution into a sort of supra-temporal fatality, an iron destiny of treachery, and despair, and endless anguish, an exuberant and flamboyantly sarcastic prelude to Orwell's final, gloomy masterpiece, *Nineteen Eighty-Four.*
—Alok Rai, *Orwell and the Politics of Despair* (Cambridge: Cambridge University Press, 1988), pp. 115–16

RICHARD I. SMYER ON THE DOUBLE ORIENTATION OF *ANIMAL FARM*

[Richard I. Smyer (b. 1935), a professor of modern literature at the University of Arizona, is the author of several books on Orwell, including *Primal Dream and Primal Crime: Orwell's Development as a Psychological Novelist* (1979) and a study of *Animal Farm* (1988), from which the following extract is taken. Here, Smyer maintains that *Animal Farm* has a double orientation: it is a political satire, but it also expresses a longing for a rustic, preindustrial world.]

The specific aim of this study is to examine the dual nature of *Animal Farm,* its bipolar orientation. On the one hand, the work calls to the attention of the contemporary reader some of the most alarming realities of a politically violent century; on the other, it offers readers an opportunity to become more emotionally and imaginatively receptive to valuable apolitical modes of experience—experience intimately connected with the reader's personal and social past. The historical past to which *Animal Farm* is designed to sensitize its readers is what Orwell considered to be on the whole the more vital, emotionally healthy, and socially cohesive and trusting world of premodern, preindustrial England—an agricultural society whose members lived in closer harmony with organic reality and natural rhythms. *Animal Farm* is doing—or attempting to do, more or less successfully—two things: at the same time that the narrative is drawing the reader into the politically satirical allegory, conjuring up scenes that hold the reader in thrall to the fable's indirect presentation of disturbing public realities, the story is also evoking in the reader's mind a sense of a pre-political self—intimations of a pastoral identity somewhere deep within the modern psyche.

The political theme of *Animal Farm* is closely associated with its satiric tone and its form as allegorical fable; the pastoral spirit of the work—its fleeting glimpses of a bucolic, somewhat idealized but not necessarily utopian rural existence—bears some kinship to the nonpoliticized animal story of the adult reader's childhood, if not his actual past. Although the English social novel has a long history, the political novel is a relatively recent phenomenon in Britain, and the tension between political message and pastoral sensibility in *Animal Farm* certainly reflects Orwell's uneasiness with the demands made by contemporary public crises on the private imagination and probably reflects the ambivalence of other British writers. Several years after writing *Animal Farm,* Orwell claimed that money used to buy rose bushes for planting was "better spent" than money for even an "excellent" Fabian research pamphlet. Of the four motives for his own writing listed in "Why I Write"— personal expression, aesthetic pleasure, the accurate description of external reality, and political persuasion—the first two are clearly nonpolitical, the third—termed a "historical impulse"—could easily relate to the public matters, and the last, the wish to exert some influence on world developments, is clearly political in intention and, it is suggested, widespread in literature. And the point stressed here is that these motives "must war against one another." The fact that in describing his work in *Animal Farm* Orwell claims only that this was the first time he had ever consciously "attempted" to unify some of these warring impulses raises the interesting possibility that this novel—rather than being a nearly finished, classically marmoreal piece of sterile perfection—is a living work still warm from its own inner conflicts and those of the age from which it was generated.

—Richard I. Smyer, Animal Farm: *Pastoralism and Politics* (Boston: Twayne, 1988), pp. 25–26

[John Rodden (b. 1956) is a professor of rhetoric at the
University of Texas. He is the author of *The Politics of
Literary Reputation* (1989), a study of Orwell's posthumous reputation from which the following extract is
taken. Here, Rodden notes that *Animal Farm*, which
was published at the very time the atomic bomb was
dropped, elicited a wide range of political opinions
from readers on different sides of the political spectrum.]

Even before Orwell's death, the political claims and counter-
claims were being lodged to both the man and the work.
Almost immediately the notoriety of *Animal Farm* turned
"Orwell" into an issue in international cultural politics.
Published in Britain in the same month (August 1945) as the
dropping of the atom bombs, *Animal Farm* exploded on the
cultural front. Orwell's little fable seemed to signal the end of
one era of East-West relations and the beginning of another:
the Cold War. One historian has judged that *Animal Farm*,
along with Arthur Koestler's *Darkness at Noon*, "probably did
more to make Western public opinion *feel* the unique Stalinist
combination of equalitarian myth and new privileges than any
historical or sociological explanation." *Animal Farm*'s plot and
characterization closely corresponded to the Russian
Revolution, its aftermath, and its principals; understandably, it
was taken—as Orwell intended—as first and foremost an
assault on the Soviet Union. Anglo-American Communist
reviewers denounced Orwell's "pig's eye view." Equally pre-
dictably, anti-Stalinist radicals in London and New York greeted
Animal Farm enthusiastically.

Quite disturbing to Orwell, however, was his fable's cele-
brated reception in conservative circles. Some conservative
reviewers read it as a criticism of the Soviet Union from the
Right; noting that it was set in England (with the lyrics of
the animal hymn "Beasts of England" modeled on the
Internationale), they welcomed it as not only anti-Stalinist but
anti-socialist, as not only pro-libertarian but pro-American. Or
they coupled Orwell with his friend Koestler as a disillusioned

former Communist Party member. Orwell reportedly told Stephen Spender that he "had not written a book against Stalin in order to provide propaganda for capitalists." Nevertheless, he fell victim to a process whose dangers he often discussed in conversation: how difficult it is, in an ideologically polarized climate, to take up any position without being presumed to hold (or being deliberately tagged with) the current string of "party line" views conventionally associated with the position. It was not well understood outside the literary Left in London and New York that Orwell was an internal critic of the Left and yet not a bitter ex-socialist.

Part of Orwell's problem was that he was now addressing a much wider audience, politically and culturally, than earlier in his career. His clear style implied a clear message. No reader needed to make a special effort to read Orwell's prose. But the plain style can mask a submerged complexity, and this was the case with the relation of Orwell's political fable to the emergent Cold War. For an allegory like *Animal Farm* which seemed so straightforward—the best example of Orwell as "The Crystal Spirit," in Woodcock's estimation—made one assume that one *did* understand the man and the book, and need not acquaint oneself with its historical-political context. The point here is not that Orwell was disingenuous or his persona false, as some radical Left critics have argued. It is simply that the man, his work, and political events so converged as to make Orwell both famous and widely misunderstood at the same time.
> —John Rodden, *The Politics of Literary Reputation: The Making and Claiming of "St. George" Orwell* (New York: Oxford University Press, 1989), pp. 23–24

MICHAEL SHELDEN ON *ANIMAL FARM* AS ORWELL'S IDEAL OF SOCIALISM

[Michael Shelden (b. 1951) is the author of biographies of Graham Greene (1994) and George Orwell (1991), from which the following extract is taken. Here, Shelden maintains that *Animal Farm* was never meant by Orwell to be simply a criticism of the Soviet Union; rather, it was intended to exemplify his ideal of a socialist state.]

As a clever satire on Stalin's betrayal of the Russian Revolution, *Animal Farm* caught the popular imagination just when the Cold War was beginning to make itself felt. For many years "anticommunists" enjoyed using it as a propaganda weapon in that war, but this was a gross misrepresentation of the book and a violation of the spirit in which Orwell wrote it. He was not a fanatical opponent of the Soviet Union. Indeed, given the fact that Stalin's agents had almost managed to imprison him in Spain, his view of the Soviet system was most enlightened. In September 1944 he explained his position to Dwight Macdonald:

> I think that if the USSR were conquered by some foreign country the working class everywhere would lose heart, for the time being at least, and the ordinary stupid capitalists who have never lost their suspicion of Russia would be encouraged. . . . I wouldn't want to see the USSR destroyed and think it ought to be defended if necessary. But I want people to become disillusioned about it and to realise that they must build their own Socialist movement without Russian interference, and I want the existence of democratic Socialism in the West to exert a regenerative influence upon Russia.

In *Animal Farm* the fat capitalist Mr. Pilkington has no more feeling for the "lower classes" he exploits than the pigs have for the "lower animals." As a model arrangement for exploitation, Animal Farm excites Pilkington's interest and prompts him to praise the pigs for their stern measures and to declare a common bond: "Between pigs and human beings there was not and there need not be any clash of interests whatever." In any case, *Animal Farm* is much more than a gloss on the failings of the Russian Revolution. It should also be seen in an earlier context. As Orwell noted, the "central idea" for the book came to him on his return from Spain, when his anger toward Stalin was balanced by his admiration for the early days of the workers' revolution in Barcelona. Simply because Stalin betrayed those Spanish workers does not mean that their revolution itself was wrong. Orwell knew what the real evil was. Five months after he finished writing *Animal Farm,* he gave readers of the *Observer* a succinct explanation of the "object-lesson" offered by the Spanish Civil War: "The Spanish war [should] be kept always in mind as an object-lesson in the folly and meanness of Power Politics."

Animal Farm affirms the values of Orwell's ideal version of socialism, making it clear that before the barnyard revolt was subjected to the treachery of the pigs, "the animals were happy as they had never conceived it possible to be." But he also makes it clear that there is no future for socialist revolutions if they look to the Soviet model for inspiration or spawn Soviet-style leaders. The book provides a powerful illustration of the consequences that must follow if such leaders are accepted. The animals allow themselves to become easy prey for Napoleon, who relentlessly accumulates power by playing on the weaknesses of his comrades. However much Orwell may have wanted it to be otherwise, he was realistic enough to see that revolutions create reactionary elements within them and that sooner or later the bright promise of early successes is obscured by attacks from those elements. The promise was still worth believing in and fighting for, but there was nothing to be gained from denying the hard realities. Writing in the *Observer* in September 1944, he remarked, "A moment always comes when the party which has seized power crushes its own Left Wing and then proceeds to disappoint the hopes with which the revolution started out."

—Michael Shelden, *Orwell: The Authorized Biography* (New York: HarperCollins, 1991), pp. 369–70

JULIAN SYMONS ON THE SIMPLICITY OF *ANIMAL FARM*

[Julian Symons (1912–1994) was a prolific British critic and novelist. Among his critical works are *Mortal Consequences* (1972), a study of the detective story,

Critical Observations (1981), and *Makers of the New: The Revolution in Literature 1912–1939* (1987). He also wrote many detective novels. In this extract, Symons asserts that the success of *Animal Farm* depends on its mixture of simplicity and sophistication.]

Animal Farm is such a total success in part because it contains no human beings, for Mr Jones the farmer is only a name. It is about animals, who are characterized with the simplicity a child might use: Major is the wise old boar, Boxer the gallant worker, frisky Clover the vain silly mare. Orwell's appreciation of animals and of natural beauty was intense, his love of the countryside and in particular of fishing and country walks something he tried awkwardly to incorporate into the pre-war novels. It emerges even in *Nineteen Eighty-Four* as he describes the lane of dappled light and shade and the ground 'misty with bluebells' down which Winston walks to meet Julia, and comes also in her description of the nearby stream with big fish in it, 'lying in the pools under the willow trees, waving their tails'. Wyndham Lewis had a comic point when he said that 'all love with Orwell takes place out of doors . . . and it is always the same woman, a sort of land-girl, who is the leading lady'. The point is made uncharitably: there was a childlike simplicity about Orwell, both in his life and his writing, which was sometimes absurd but more often attractive, and in *Animal Farm* the blend of sophistication and simplicity in his nature led him to produce a perfect work of art.

By his own account the story had its origins when he saw a small boy driving a cart-horse along a narrow track. As the boy whipped the horse when it tried to turn, Orwell thought that if such animals became aware of their strength human beings would no longer have power over them. Perhaps something like that incident occurred (Orwell was not always literally accurate in such matters), but really the basis of the fable lay in the writer's personality. ⟨. . .⟩

The charm of the manner and the perfection of the story are undoubted, but a question remains: what is being told us in this allegory, what understanding are we meant to take away from it? The simplest answer is that given by the political Right-wingers already mentioned, who have done their best to appropriate Orwell as a prophet whose message was that to disturb the social order always ends in totalitarian dictatorship. That, however, is certainly not the reading of his work Orwell intended. Shortly before his death, much distressed by the way in which American reviewers in particular had greeted *Nineteen Eighty-Four* as a polemic against all kinds of Socialism, he issued a statement specifically praising the liberal attitudes and intentions of the British Labour Party government of the time (1949), a statement which was generally ignored. It should not have been disregarded. Orwell remained a Socialist until his death, and *Animal Farm* was not meant to be a parable giving comfort to the Right wing.

—Julian Symons, "Introduction" to *Animal Farm* (New York: Knopf, 1993), pp. xix–xxi

Works by George Orwell

Down and Out in Paris and London. 1933.

Burmese Days. 1934.

A Clergyman's Daughter. 1935.

Keep the Aspidistra Flying. 1936.

The Road to Wigan Pier. 1937.

Homage to Catalonia. 1938.

Coming Up for Air. 1939.

Inside the Whale and Other Essays. 1940.

The Lion and the Unicorn: Socialism and the English Genius. 1941.

Talking to India. (editor) 1943.

Animal Farm: A Fairy Story. 1945.

Critical Essays (Dickens, Dali and Others). 1946.

James Burnham and the Managerial Revolution. 1946.

The English People. 1947.

Politics and the English Language. 1947.

British Pamphleteers I: From the Sixteenth Century to the French Revolution (editor; with Reginald Reynolds). 1948.

Nineteen Eighty-four. 1949.

Shooting an Elephant and Other Essays. 1950.

England, Your England and Other Essays. 1953.

Collected Essays. 1961.

Collected Essays, Journalism and Letters. Ed. Sonia Orwell and Ian Angus. 1968. 4 vols.

Ten Animal Farm Letters to His Agent, Leonard Moore. Ed. Michael Shelden. 1984.

The War Broadcasts. Ed. W. J. West. 1985.

The War Commentaries. Ed. W. J. West. 1985.

Works about George Orwell and Animal Farm

Alldritt, Keith. *The Making of George Orwell.* New York: St. Martin's Press, 1969.

Atkins, John. *George Orwell: A Literary Study.* 2nd ed. London: Calder & Boyars, 1971.

Auden, W. H. "W. H. Auden on George Orwell." *Spectator,* 16 January 1971, pp. 86–87.

Buitenhuis, Peter, ed. *George Orwell: A Reassessment.* New York: St. Martin's Press, 1988.

Carter, Michael. *George Orwell and the Problem of Authentic Existence.* Totowa, NJ: Barnes & Noble, 1985.

Carter, Thomas. "Group Psychology Phenomena of a Political System as Satirized in *Animal Farm:* An Application of the Theories of W. R. Bion." *Human Relations* 27 (1974): 525–46.

Connelly, Mark. *The Diminished Self: Orwell and the Loss of Freedom.* Pittsburgh: Duquesne University Press, 1987.

Cook, Timothy. "Upton Sinclair's *The Jungle* and Orwell's *Animal Farm:* A Relationship Explored." *Modern Fiction Studies* 30 (1984): 696–703.

Crick, Bernard R. *George Orwell: A Life.* Boston: Little, Brown, 1980.

Davis, Robert Murray. "Politics in the Pig-Pen." *Journal of Popular Culture* 2 (1968): 314–20.

Elbarbary, Samir. "Language as Theme in *Animal Farm.*" *International Fiction Review* 19 (1992): 31–38.

Fergenson, Laraine. "George Orwell's *Animal Farm:* A Twentieth-Century Fable." *Bestia* 2 (May 1990): 109–18.

Greer, Herb. "Orwell in Perspective." *Commentary* 75, No. 3 (March 1983): 50–54.

Gross, Miriam, ed. *The World of George Orwell.* London: Weidenfeld & Nicolson, 1971.

Hunter, Lynette. *George Orwell: The Search for a Voice.* Milton Keynes, UK: Open University Press, 1984.

Knapp, John. "Dance to a Creepy Minuet: Orwell's *Burmese Days,* Precursor to *Animal Farm." Modern Fiction Studies* 21 (1975): 11–29.

Leavens, Dennis. "Finding One to Worship, Finding One to Betray: The Language of Fable in Thurber, Orwell, and Pynchon." *Bestia* 3 (May 1991): 74–86.

Lee, Robert A. "The Uses of Form: A Reading of *Animal Farm." Studies in Short Fiction* 6 (1969): 557–73.

Lewis, Anthony. "T. S. Eliot and *Animal Farm." New York Times Book Review,* 26 January 1969, pp. 14, 16.

Lewis, Wyndham. "Orwell, or Two and Two Make Four." In Lewis's *The Writer and the Absolute.* London: Methuen, 1952, pp. 153–94.

Lief, Ruth Ann. *Homage to Oceania: The Prophetic Vision of George Orwell.* Columbus: Ohio State University Press, 1969.

Meyers, Jeffrey. "Orwell's Bestiary: The Political Allegory of *Animal Farm." Studies in the Twentieth Century* 8 (1971): 65–84.

—————. *A Reader's Guide to George Orwell.* London: Thames & Hudson, 1975.

Meyers, Valerie. *George Orwell.* New York: St. Martin's Press, 1991.

Mezciems, Jenny. "Swift and Orwell: Utopia as Nightmare." In *Between Dream and Nature: Essays on Utopia and Dystopia,* ed. Dominic Baker-Smith and C. C. Barfoot. Amsterdam: Rodopi, 1987, pp. 91–112.

Modern Fiction Studies 21, No. 1 (Spring 1975). Special George Orwell issue.

Paden, Frances Freeman. "Narrative Dynamics in *Animal Farm." Literature in Performance* 5, No. 2 (April 1985): 49–55.

Reilly, Patrick. *George Orwell: The Age's Adversity.* New York: St. Martin's Press, 1986.

Sandison, Alan. *The Last Man in Europe: An Essay on George Orwell.* New York: Barnes & Noble, 1974.

Slater, Ian. *Orwell: The Road to Airstrip One.* New York: Norton, 1985.

Smyer, Richard I. "*Animal Farm:* The Burden of Consciousness." *English Language Notes* 9 (1971): 55–59.

————. *Primal Dream and Primal Crime: Orwell's Development as a Psychological Novelist.* Columbia: University of Missouri Press, 1979.

Solomon, Robert. "Ant Farm: An Orwellian Allegory." In *Reflections on America, 1984: An Orwell Symposium,* ed. Robert Mulvihill. Athens: University of Georgia Press, 1986, pp. 114–29.

Stansky, Peter, and William Abrahams. *Orwell, the Transformation.* New York: Knopf, 1980.

————. *The Unknown Orwell.* New York: Knopf, 1972.

Todorov, Tzvetan. "Politics, Morality, and the Writer's Life: Notes on George Orwell." *Stanford French Review* 16 (1992): 136–42.

Voorhees, Richard. *The Paradox of George Orwell.* West Lafayette, IN: Purdue University Press, 1961.

Warburg, Fredric. *All Authors Are Equal.* London: Hutchinson, 1973.

Watson, George. "Orwell's Nazi Renegade." *Sewanee Review* 94 (1986): 486–95.

Williams, Raymond. *George Orwell.* New York: Viking Press, 1971.

Wykes, David. *A Preface to Orwell.* London: Longman, 1987.

Zwerdling, Alex. "Orwell: Socialism v. Pessimism." *New Review* 1 (June 1974): 5–17.

Index of
Themes and Ideas